Henry and the Bullfrog

STORY BY **ANGELA CASTILLO**
ILLUSTRATED BY **CHER JIANG**
CONTRIBUTOR **HAIYING WU**

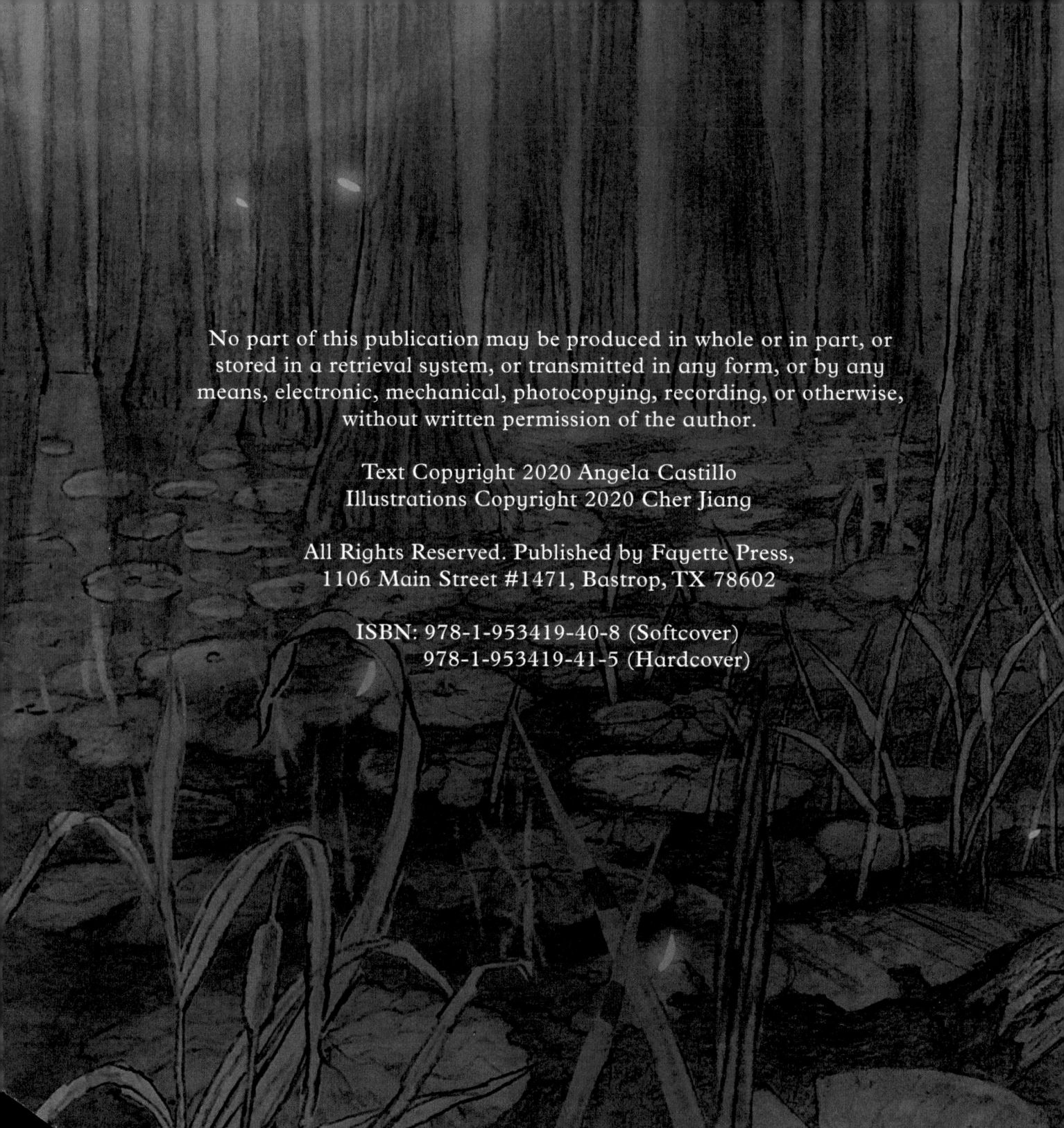

No part of this publication may be produced in whole or in part, or stored in a retrieval system, or transmitted in any form, or by any means, electronic, mechanical, photocopying, recording, or otherwise, without written permission of the author.

Text Copyright 2020 Angela Castillo
Illustrations Copyright 2020 Cher Jiang

All Rights Reserved. Published by Fayette Press,
1106 Main Street #1471, Bastrop, TX 78602

ISBN: 978-1-953419-40-8 (Softcover)
978-1-953419-41-5 (Hardcover)

Saturday night arrived. Animals gathered around a little pond in a wood. They found comfy places to sit. Quiet clouds drifted across the cool white moon. Soon, the most wonderful sounds began.

First, the Peeper Brothers began to peep.
As they sang, little bubbles rose on their throats.

Cricket warmed up his wings. His chirps blended perfectly with the symphony of animal sounds.

Lady Loon opened her beak. Her soprano trill reached to the stars.

The animal audience held its breath, waiting.
Where was the star of the show?

A large, blobby creature emerged from the water.

He lumbered up onto a lily pad.

Bullfrog gave his musical friends a broad, froggy grin, then took a deep breath, swelling up with lots of swampy air.

Out a song came, deep and powerful. It shook the animals to their furry and scaly toes.

When the show was over, the animals sighed happily. Another wonderful concert.

The next Saturday night, Lady Loon, the Peeper Brothers, Cricket, and Bullfrog sang together again.

Something crashed through the cattails.
A bright light shone in the animals' eyes.

All the creatures scattered for dens and trees, holes, and hollow logs.

"What a great frog," said the boy, whose name was Henry. He scooped him up with gentle hands and put him in a big jar. "I believe I'll take him home and keep him."

Bullfrog stared out of the jar with big eyes. But he didn't croak a word.

Henry found an empty tank. He poured in some pond water. Then he put in some nice, flat stones for Bullfrog to sit on. "Now you can sing for me."

But Bullfrog couldn't sing. He was too sad.

Henry caught earthworms and minnows.
He gave them to Bullfrog.
"Maybe after you eat, you will sing."
But Bullfrog wouldn't sing. He was too sad.

Back at the pond, Cricket, Lady Loon, and the Peeper Brothers had an emergency meeting. "We have to save Bullfrog!" said Cricket, stomping his little brown foot.

"Yes, yes!" shouted the Peeper Brothers.

"I have a plan," said Lady Loon.

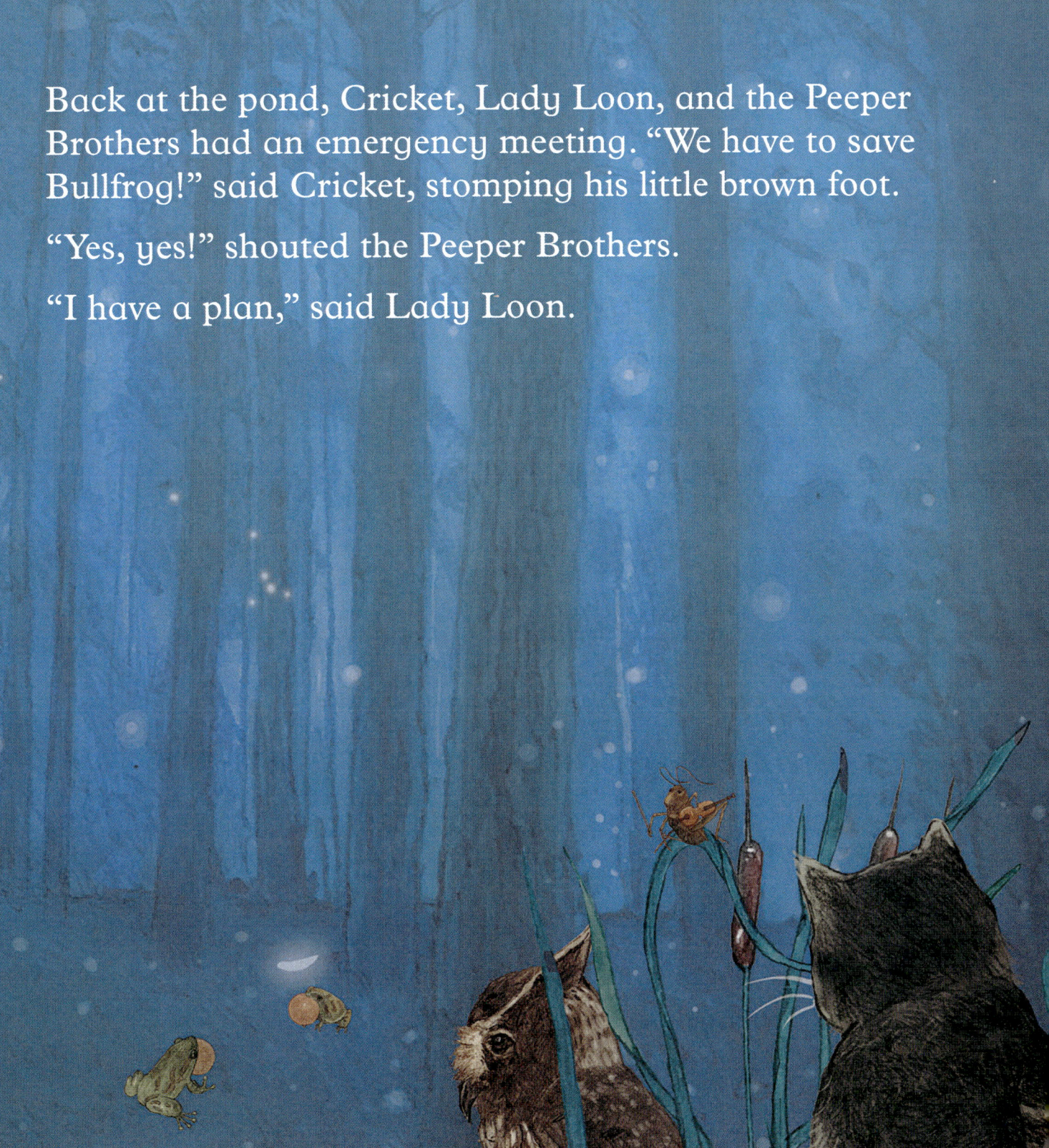

The next Saturday night, Henry moved Bullfrog's tank to the window and placed it in the moonlight. Bullfrog squatted in the corner, his big eyes shut tight.

"Please sing a song!" Henry begged.

Suddenly, outside the window, Henry heard an impossible sound. Peepers and a cricket playing a melody! The voice of a loon rose up. Somehow, Henry could understand the words.

"Please, please, let Bullfrog go,
he's such a dear friend, you know.
Please, please, let him be free,
he'll sing again, you will see."

Henry stared out into the yard. He couldn't see the animals, but he could hear them. All at once, the yips of foxes, hoots of owls, and the chirrups of raccoons swelled into the night. Dozens and dozens of forest creatures added their voices.

*"Please, please, let him be free,
he'll sing again, you will see."*

Bullfrog crept nearer to the glass, his eyes wide, searching.

Henry sighed. "I guess I'd better let you go," he said to Bullfrog.

Once more, he scooped him up. This time, he opened the window, and carefully placed him outside on the grass.

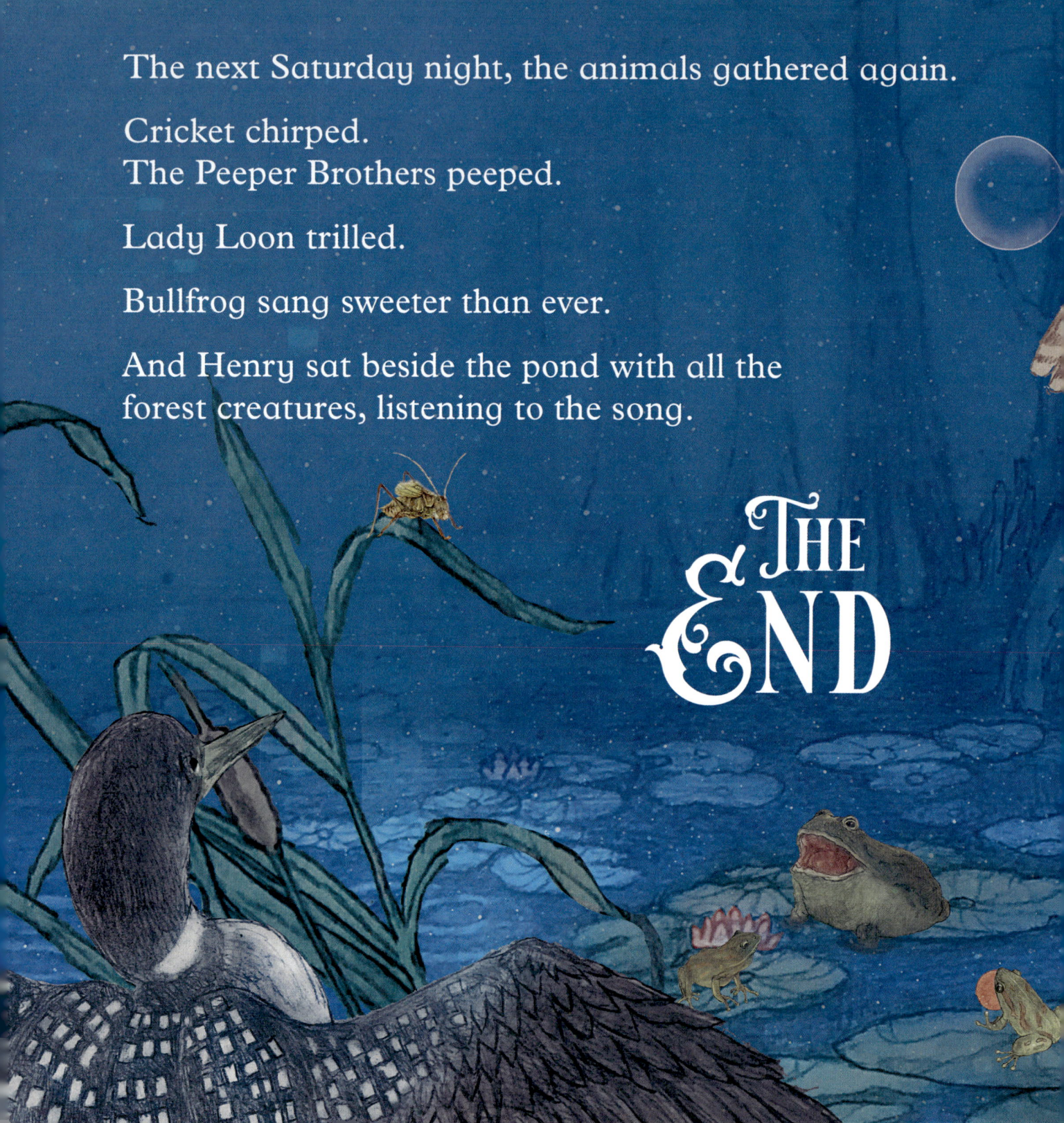

The next Saturday night, the animals gathered again.

Cricket chirped.
The Peeper Brothers peeped.

Lady Loon trilled.

Bullfrog sang sweeter than ever.

And Henry sat beside the pond with all the forest creatures, listening to the song.

THE END

Animal Facts

Bullfrogs

The largest bullfrog in the world is the Goliath frog.

Specimens have been found that are up to 13 inches (33 centimeters) in length and weigh up to 7.2 pounds (3.25 kilograms). American bullfrogs can weigh up to 1.5 pounds, which is still a pretty big frog.

American bullfrogs can live up to ten years in the wild, and sometimes sixteen years in captivity.

Bullfrogs start off as tadpoles, then later metamorphosis into adults. They can stay as tadpoles for up to four years in cold environments.

Rainbow Snake

The rainbow snake eats a large variety of animals such as frogs, worms and fish when young. However, adults dine only on the American eel. So if you want to find a rainbow snake, you'll have to find American eels first!

Since this snake isn't venomous, it pokes its tail at predators to try to get away. Its tail is not sharp and cannot harm humans in any way.

Gray Fox

Most gray foxes grow to be about three feet long, with their tail making up one-third of their body length.

Gray foxes possess extremely long, sharp claws that help them dig dens, and also climb trees. They are the only breed of fox that can climb trees.

Common Loon

Loons can make a variety of sounds, from their signature mournful cry, to wolf-like whines.

Loons have an awkward walk on land, but in the water they can dive almost 200 feet. One of the reasons they can do this is because their bodies have internal air sacks to store oxygen.

Baby loons are called chicks. They can swim almost immediately after hatching, and enjoy going for a ride on their parents' backs.

Raccoon

In the wintertime, raccoons spend much of their time sleeping, though they don't officially hibernate. They live off stored fat and can lose up to 50 percent of their body weight.

Raccoons can fall up to 40 feet without being hurt.

Spring Peepers

Spring peepers belong to a group of frogs known as chorus frogs and are found from northern Florida up to Canada.

The noise spring peepers make is similar to a ringing bell and is actually part of a courtship ritual where the males call out to the females of the species.

Crickets

Only male crickets can chirp. They do this by rubbing their wings together.

Crickets can lay up to 2,000 eggs at once. That's a lot of crickets!

Crickets are found almost all over the world, and there are over 900 species.

Great Horned Owl

Though baby owls can fly at ten weeks old, the parents still care for them and feed them for several months.

The great horned owl is the second largest owl in North America, next only to the snowy owl.

Find more of Angela's books, including her books for kids, on Amazon at

www.amazon.com/Angela-Castillo/e/B00CJUELT0

Find fun, free activities and more at
http://tobythetrilby.weebly.com

Made in the USA
Middletown, DE
20 February 2022